The World's Greatest
KNOCK
KNOCK
JOKES
for Kids!

BOB PHILLIPS

HARVEST HOUSE PUBLISHERS
Eugene, Oregon 97402

THE WORLD'S GREATEST KNOCK-KNOCK JOKES FOR KIDS
Copyright © 2000 by Bob Phillips
Published by Harvest House Publishers
Eugene, Oregon 97402

ISBN: 0-7369-0273-2

Printed in the United States of America.

04 05 06 07 08 09 / BC / 18 17 16 15 14 13 12 11 10

Contents

Adventure

Knock, knock.
Who's there?
Gretta.
Gretta who?
Gretta long, little doggie, gretta long.

Knock, knock.
Who's there?
Sybil.
Sybil who?
Sybil Simon met a pieman going to the fair.

Knock, knock.
Who's there?
Zing.
Zing who?
Zing a song of sixpence...

❖ ❖ ❖

Knock, knock.
Who's there?
Eileen.
Eileen who?
Eileen on a walking stick.

❖ ❖ ❖

Knock, knock.
Who's there?
Zippy.
Zippy who?
Zippy dee doo dah...zippy dee ay...

❖ ❖ ❖

Knock, knock.
Who's there?
Yee.
Yee who?
Yeehaw—ride 'em cowboy!

❖ ❖ ❖

Knock, knock.
Who's there?
K-9.
K-9 who?
K-9, B-6, O-74, I-24, N-52—BINKO!

❖ ❖ ❖

Knock, knock.
Who's there?
Wayne.
Wayne who?
Wayne drops keep falling on my head

❖ ❖ ❖

Knock, knock.
Who's there?
Victor.
Victor who?
Victor his pants on the fence.

❖ ❖ ❖

Knock, knock.
Who's there?
Robot.
Robot who?
Robot don't splash with the oars.

❖ ❖ ❖

Knock, knock.
Who's there?
Verdi.
Verdi who?
Verdi been all day?

❖ ❖ ❖

Knock, knock.
Who's there?
Uriah.
Uriah who?
Keep Uriah on the ball.

❖ ❖ ❖

Knock, knock.
Who's there?
Telly.
Telly who?
Tellyscope.

❖ ❖ ❖

Knock, knock.
Who's there?
Sloane.
Sloane who?
Sloane Ranger rides again.

Knock, knock.
Who's there?
Shelby.
Shelby who?
Shelby comin' 'round the mountain when she comes...

Knock, knock.
Who's there?
Saber.
Saber who?
Saber, she's drowning!

Knock, knock.
Who's there?
Ron.
Ron who?
Ron faster, there's a tiger after us!

Knock, knock.
Who's there?
Romeo.
Romeo who?
Romeo cross the lake in a canoe.

❖ ❖ ❖

Knock, knock.
Who's there?
Randy.
Randy who?
Randy four-minute mile!

Knock, knock.
Who's there?
Owl.
Owl who?
Owl aboard.

❖ ❖ ❖

Knock, knock.
Who's there?
Orson.
Orson who?
Orson wagon are parked outside.

Knock, knock.
Who's there?
Mickey.
Mickey who?
Mickey is stuck in the lock.

❖ ❖ ❖

Knock, knock.
Who's there?
Marcella.
Marcella who?
Marcella's full of water. Call a plumber.

❖ ❖ ❖

Knock, knock.
Who's there?
Lyndon.
Lyndon who?
Lyndon Bridge is falling down.

❖ ❖ ❖

Knock, knock.
Who's there?
Luke.
Luke who?
Luke through the keyhole and see.

❖ ❖ ❖

Knock, knock.
Who's there?
Ken.
Ken who?
Ken I come in? It's very cold out here.

❖ ❖ ❖

Knock, knock.
Who's there?
Kayak.
Kayak who?
Kayak if you want to.

❖ ❖ ❖

Knock, knock.
Who's there?
Justin.
Justin who?
Justin time for dinner.

❖ ❖ ❖

Knock, knock.
Who's there?
Juicy.
Juicy who?
Juicy any ghosts in that haunted house?

Knock, knock.
Who's there?
John.
John who?
John your marks, get set, go!

❖ ❖ ❖

Knock, knock.
Who's there?
José.
José who?
José can you see by the dawn's early light?

❖ ❖ ❖

Knock, knock.
Who's there?
Jethro.
Jethro who?
Jethro the canoe and stop talking.

❖ ❖ ❖

Knock, knock.
Who's there?
Habit.
Habit who?
Habit your way.

❖ ❖ ❖

Knock, knock.
Who's there?
Fire engine.
Fire engine who?
Fire engine one and prepare for blast-off.

And They Say...

Knock, knock.
Who's there?
Carrot.
Carrot who?
Carrot me back to old Virginny.

Knock, knock.
Who's there?
Yule.
Yule who?
Yule come on down now, ya hear!

14

Knock, knock.
Who's there?
Yachts.
Yachts who?
Yachts up, Doc?

Knock, knock.
Who's there?
X.
X who?
X-tra, X-tra, read all about it!

Knock, knock.
Who's there?
Wendy.
Wendy who?
Wendy red, red robin comes bob, bob, bobbin' along.

Knock, knock.
Who's there?
Weirdo.
Weirdo who?
Weirdo you think you're going?

Knock, knock.
Who's there?
Weasel.
Weasel who?
Weasel while you work.

Knock, knock.
Who's there?
Watson.
Watson who?
Nothing much, Watson with you?

Knock, knock.
Who's there?
Utica.
Utica who?
Utica high road, and I'll take the low road.

Knock, knock.
Who's there?
Tom.
Tom who?
Tom-orrow is another day.

Knock, knock.
Who's there?
Toby.
Toby who?
Toby or not Toby, that is the question...

Knock, knock.
Who's there?
Tibet.
Tibet who?
Early Tibet and early to rise, makes a man healthy, wealthy, and wise.

Knock, knock.
Who's there?
Shirley.
Shirley who?
Shirley you must be joking!

Knock, knock.
Who's there?
Sharon.
Sharon who?
Sharon share alike.

❖ ❖ ❖

Knock, knock.
Who's there?
Saul.
Saul who?
Saul in your head.

❖ ❖ ❖

Knock, knock.
Who's there?
Sahara.
Sahara who?
Sahara you today?

❖ ❖ ❖

Knock, knock.
Who's there?
Quacker.
Quacker who?
Quacker 'nother knock-knock joke before I leave.

❖ ❖ ❖

Knock, knock.
Who's there?
Kerch.
Kerch who?
Gesundheit!

❖ ❖ ❖

Knock, knock.
Who's there?
Holly.
Holly who?
Hollylujah.

❖ ❖ ❖

Knock, knock.
Who's there?
Hiram.
Hiram who?
Hiram fine. How are you?

❖ ❖ ❖

Knock, knock.
Who's there?
Hatch.
Hatch who?
God bless you!

❖ ❖ ❖

Knock, knock.
Who's there?
Hair.
Hair who?
Hair today, gone tomorrow.

❖ ❖ ❖

Knock, knock.
Who's there?
Fang.
Fang who?
Fang you very much for answering the door.

❖ ❖ ❖

Knock, knock.
Who's there?
Ether.
Ether who?
Ether Bunny.

❖ ❖ ❖

Knock, knock.
Who's there?
Estelle.
Estelle who?
Estelle more Ether Bunny jokes?

❖ ❖ ❖

Knock, knock.
Who's there?
Elsie.
Elsie who?
Elsie you around.

Knock, knock.
Who's there?
Edsel.
Edsel who?
Edsel there is, there ain't no more.

Knock, knock.
Who's there?
Dewey.
Dewey who?
Dewey have to keep telling knock-knock jokes?

Knock, knock.
Who's there?
Column.
Column who?
Column loud and clear.

Knock, knock.
Who's there?
Castro.
Castro who?
Castro bread upon the waters.

Knock, knock.
Who's there?
Arch.
Arch who?
Bless you!

Knock, knock.
Who's there?
Hair combs.
Hair combs who?
Hair combs the judge! Hair combs the judge!

Animal Crack-Ups

Knock, knock.
Who's there?
Polly Warner.
Polly Warner who?
Polly Warner cracker?

❖ ❖ ❖

Knock, knock.
Who's there?
Willoughby.
Willoughby who?
Willoughby a monkey's uncle.

❖ ❖ ❖

Knock, knock.
Who's there?
Vel.
Vel who?
Vel, how's my dog doing?

❖ ❖ ❖

Knock, knock.
Who's there?
Seymour.
Seymour who?
I seymour kittens out here!

❖ ❖ ❖

Knock, knock.
Who's there?
Hop.
Hop who?
Hop, hop away—the Easter Bunny's gone!

❖ ❖ ❖

Knock, knock.
Who's there?
Samoa.
Samoa who?
Samoa Easter bunnies.

❖ ❖ ❖

Knock, knock.
Who's there?
Gopher.
Gopher who?
Gopher your gun, Sheriff!

Knock, knock.
Who's there?
Gorilla.
Gorilla who?
Gorilla my dreams, I love you.

Knock, knock.
Who's there?
Dogs.
Dogs who?
No they don't. Dogs bark.

Knock, knock.
Who's there?
Don.
Don who?
Don-key. Hee-haw.

Knock, knock.
Who's there?
Etta.
Etta who?
Etta cat yesterday. It was gross.

Knock, knock.
Who's there?
Cock-a-doodle.
Cock-a-doodle who?
Are you a rooster?

Knock, knock.
Who's there?
Clark.
Clark who?
Clark, clark, clark—I'm a chicken.

Knock, knock.
Who's there?
Cow.
Cow who?
Cow says moo, not who!

Knock, knock.
Who's there?
Albee.
Albee who?
Albee a monkey's uncle!

Knock, knock.
Who's there?
Althea.
Althea who?
Althea later, alligator!

Knock, knock.
Who's there?
Ammonia.
Ammonia who?
Ammonia bird in a gilded cage.

Knock, knock.
Who's there?
Amos.
Amos who?
Amos-quito bit me.

Knock, knock.
Who's there?
Andy.
Andy who?
Andy bit me again.

Knock, knock.
Who's there?
Annie.
Annie who?
Annie-body seen my lost dog?

Knock, knock.
Who's there?
Beehive.
Beehive who?
Beehive yourself or you will get into trouble.

Knock, knock.
Who's there?
Consumption.
Consumption who?
Consumption be done about all these Easter
    bunnies?

Watch Out!

Knock, knock.
Who's there?
Midas.
Midas who?
Midas well relax. I'm not going away.

Knock, knock.
Who's there?
Adair.
Adair who?
Adair you to open this door!

Knock, knock.
Who's there?
Yukon.
Yukon who?
Yukon too many people.

Knock, knock.
Who's there?
Wendy.
Wendy who?
Wendy joke is over, you had better laugh.

Knock, knock.
Who's there?
Wash Out.
Wash Out who?
Wash Out, I'm coming in!

Knock, knock.
Who's there?
Thumping.
Thumping who?
Thumping green and slimy is crawling on your
    shoulder.

Knock, knock.
Who's there?
Thistle.
Thistle who?
Thistle not be the last time I knock on your door.

Knock, knock.
Who's there?
Thesis.
Thesis who?
Thesis a stickup!

Knock, knock.
Who's there?
Stella.
Stella who?
Stella 'nother crazy knock-knock joke.

Knock, knock.
Who's there?
Stan.
Stan who?
Stan back quick—I think I'm going to be sick.

Knock, knock.
Who's there?
Rufus.
Rufus who?
Rufus leaking and I'm getting wet.

Knock, knock.
Who's there?
Razor.
Razor who?
Razor hands. This is a stick-up.

Knock, knock.
Who's there?
Radio.
Radio who?
Radio not, here I come.

Knock, knock.
Who's there?
Panther.
Panther who?
Panther falling down 'cause I need a belt.

Knock, knock.
Who's there?
Owl.
Owl who?
Owl be seeing you!

Knock, knock.
Who's there?
Nod.
Nod who?
Nod you again!

Knock, knock.
Who's there?
Miniature.
Miniature who?
Miniature open your mouth, you might put your
    foot in it.

Knock, knock.
Who's there?
Thistle.
Thistle who?
Thistle teach you to ask silly questions.

Knock, knock.
Who's there?
Megan.
Megan who?
Megan end to these knock-knock jokes before I
   knock-knock you!

Knock, knock.
Who's there?
Manuel.
Manuel who?
Manuel be sorry if you don't unlock the door!

Knock, knock.
Who's there?
Made-ja.
Made-ja who?
Made-ja open the door!

❖ ❖ ❖

Knock, knock.
Who's there?
Lindy.
Lindy who?
Lindy some money, please?

❖ ❖ ❖

Knock, knock.
Who's there?
Lessen.
Lessen who?
Lessen now and I'll tell you another knock-knock
　　joke.

❖ ❖ ❖

Knock, knock.
Who's there?
Izzy.
Izzy who?
Izzy come, Izzy go.

❖ ❖ ❖

Knock, knock.
Who's there?
Hugh Maid.
Hugh Maid who?
Hugh Maid your bed, now lie in it!

❖ ❖ ❖

Knock, knock.
Who's there?
Hannah.
Hannah who?
Hannah over all your money. This is a holdup!

❖ ❖ ❖

Knock, knock.
Who's there?
Egypt.
Egypt who?
Egypt me—call the police!

❖ ❖ ❖

Knock, knock.
Who's there?
Dishes.
Dishes who?
Dishes not the end of my knock-knock jokes.

❖ ❖ ❖

Knock, knock.
Who's there?
Diesel.
Diesel who?
Diesel be your last chance to open the door.

❖ ❖ ❖

Knock, knock.
Who's there?
Handover.
Handover who?
Handover your money, this is a stickup!

❖ ❖ ❖

Knock, knock.
Who's there?
Datsun.
Datsun who?
Datsun of mine is sure a little pest!

❖ ❖ ❖

Knock, knock.
Who's there?
Amana.
Amana who?
Amana very bad mood.

❖ ❖ ❖

Knock, knock.
Who's there?
Egypt.
Egypt who?
Egypt me and I want my mummy back.

❖ ❖ ❖

Knock, knock.
Who's there?
Armen.
Armen who?
Armen every word I say.

Knock, knock.
Who's there?
B.C.
B.C. who?
B.C.-ing you!

Check Again

Knock, knock.
Who's there?
Viola.
Viola who?
Viola sudden you don't remember me?

Knock, knock.
Who's there?
Tibet.
Tibet who?
Tibet you can't guess who's knocking at the door.

Knock, knock.
Who's there?
Thermos.
Thermos who?
Thermos be someone who feels the way I do.

Knock, knock.
Who's there?
Thatcher.
Thatcher who?
Thatcher was a funny joke.

Knock, knock.
Who's there?
Tank.
Tank who?
Tank you for coming to the door.

Knock, knock.
Who's there?
Stan.
Stan who?
Stan aside—I'm coming through.

Knock, knock.
Who's there?
Sherwood.
Sherwood who?
Sherwood like to hear another knock-knock joke.

Knock, knock.
Who's there?
Sari.
Sari who?
Sari I was sarong!

Knock, knock.
Who's there?
Raymond.
Raymond who?
Raymond me to buy milk!

Knock, knock.
Who's there?
Orange juice.
Orange juice who?
Orange juice going to let me come in?

Knock, knock.
Who's there?
Omelet.
Omelet who?
Omelet smarter than I look!

Knock, knock.
Who's there?
Omega.
Omega who?
Omega better jokes than these, please!

Knock, knock.
Who's there?
Omar.
Omar who?
Omar goodness! I must have knocked on the wrong
    door.

Knock, knock.
Who's there?
Neil.
Neil who?
Neil and pray!

Knock, knock.
Who's there?
Mississippi.
Mississippi who?
Mississippi and Mr. Sippy. May we come in?

Knock, knock.
Who's there?
Midas.
Midas who?
Midas well try again...
Knock, knock.
Who's there?
Midas.
Midas who?
Midas well open the door and find out.

❖ ❖ ❖

Knock, knock.
Who's there?
Me.
Me who?
Don't you know your own name?

❖ ❖ ❖

Knock, knock.
Who's there?
Mae.
Mae who?
Mae-be I'll tell you, and Mae-be I won't!

Knock, knock.
Who's there?
Orange.
Orange who?
Orange you glad there are knock-knock jokes?

Knock, knock.
Who's there?
Lotto.
Lotto who?
Lotto good that will do.

Knock, knock.
Who's there?
Kent.
Kent who?
Kent you just wait until I tell you another knock-knock joke?

❖ ❖ ❖

Knock, knock.
Who's there?
Jess.
Jess who?
Jess a friend of yours.

❖ ❖ ❖

Knock, knock.
Who's there?
Isadore.
Isadore who?
Isadore locked?

❖ ❖ ❖

Knock, knock.
Who's there?
Isabel.
Isabel who?
Isabel out of order?

❖ ❖ ❖

Knock, knock.
Who's there?
Hugo.
Hugo who?
Hugo your way, and I'll go mine!

❖ ❖ ❖

Knock, knock.
Who's there?
House.
House who?
House it going?

❖ ❖ ❖

Knock, knock.
Who's there?
Howard.
Howard who?
Howard you today?

❖ ❖ ❖

Knock, knock.
Who's there?
Jess.
Jess who?
Jess little old me.

❖ ❖ ❖

Knock, knock.
Who's there?
Hewlett.
Hewlett who?
Hewlett the cat out of the bag?

❖ ❖ ❖

Knock, knock.
Who's there?
Foreign.
Foreign who?
Foreign 20 blackbirds baked in a pie.

❖ ❖ ❖

Knock, knock.
Who's there?
Emerson.
Emerson who?
Emerson nice shoes you've got on.

❖ ❖ ❖

Knock, knock.
Who's there?
Isabel.
Isabel who?
Isabel ringing?

❖ ❖ ❖

Knock, knock.
Who's there?
Diesel.
Diesel who?
Diesel all make you laugh if you aren't very bright!

❖ ❖ ❖

Knock, knock.
Who's there?
Della.
Della who?
Della Katessen.

❖ ❖ ❖

Knock, knock.
Who's there?
Chester.
Chester who?
Chester minute and I'll see.

❖ ❖ ❖

Knock, knock.
Who's there?
Dishes.
Dishes who?
Dishes me. Who ish you?

❖ ❖ ❖

Knock, knock.
Who's there?
Isabella.
Isabella who?
Isabella don't work—that's why I'm knocking.

Doesn't Hurt to Ask

Knock, knock.
Who's there?
Woody.
Woody who?
Woody open the door, please?

Knock, knock.
Who's there?
Wooden.
Wooden who?
Wooden nickel buy me that piece of candy?

Knock, knock.
Who's there?
Wilda.
Wilda who?
Wilda movie be on TV tonight?

❖ ❖ ❖

Knock, knock.
Who's there?
Tulsa.
Tulsa who?
Tulsa story, please.

❖ ❖ ❖

Knock, knock.
Who's there?
Sherwood.
Sherwood who?
Sherwood like to come in.

❖ ❖ ❖

Knock, knock.
Who's there?
Senior.
Senior who?
Senior uncle lately?

❖ ❖ ❖

Knock, knock.
Who's there?
Popeye.
Popeye who?
Popeye've got to have the car tonight.

Knock, knock.
Who's there?
Police.
Police who?
Police may I sit down?

Knock, knock.
Who's there?
Oscar.
Oscar who?
Oscar for a date!

Knock, knock.
Who's there?
Osborn.
Osborn who?
Osborn today. When were you born?

Knock, knock.
Who's there?
Orange.
Orange who?
Orange you even going to open the door?

Knock, knock.
Who's there?
Ooze.
Ooze who?
Ooze the person in charge around here?

Knock, knock.
Who's there?
Noah.
Noah who?
Noah good place to eat around here?

Knock, knock.
Who's there?
Needle.
Needle who?
Needle little money for the movies.

Knock, knock.
Who's there?
Max.
Max who?
Max no difference. Let me in.

Knock, knock.
Who's there?
Gillette.
Gillette who?
Gillette the cat out?

Knock, knock.
Who's there?
Eddie.
Eddie who?
Eddie-body home?

Knock, knock.
Who's there?
Dewey.
Dewey who?
Dewey have to listen to all this knocking?

Knock, knock.
Who's there?
Desdemona.
Desdemona who?
Desdemona Lisa still hang on the gallery wall?

Knock, knock.
Who's there?
Consumption.
Consumption who?
Consumption be done about these knock-knock
    jokes?

Knock, knock.
Who's there?
Chimney.
Chimney who?
Chimney cricket! Have you seen Pinocchio?

Knock, knock.
Who's there?
Archer.
Archer who?
Archer glad to see me?

❖ ❖ ❖

Knock, knock.
Who's there?
Canoe.
Canoe who?
Canoe come out and play with me?

❖ ❖ ❖

Knock, knock.
Who's there?
Bob.
Bob who?
Bob baa black sheep have you any wool?

❖ ❖ ❖

Knock, knock.
Who's there?
Agatha.
Agatha who?
Agatha feeling you're fooling me.

❖ ❖ ❖

Knock, knock.
Who's there?
Amis.
Amis who?
Amis is as good as a mile.

Knock, knock.
Who's there?
Canoe.
Canoe who?
Canoe help me with my homework?

Knock, knock.
Who's there?
Annapolis.
Annapolis who?
Annapolis what keeps the doctor away.

Knock, knock.
Who's there?
Arthur.
Arthur who?
Arthur any jobs available?

❖ ❖ ❖

Knock, knock.
Who's there?
Avenue.
Avenue who?
Avenue answered this door before?

❖ ❖ ❖

Knock, knock.
Who's there?
Aware.
Aware who?
Aware, aware have my little sheep gone?

❖ ❖ ❖

Knock, knock.
Who's there?
Ax.
Ax who?
Ax your mother if you can come out and play.

❖ ❖ ❖

Knock, knock.
Who's there?
Barbara.
Barbara who?
Barbara black sheep have you any wool?

❖ ❖ ❖

Knock, knock.
Who's there?
Cain.
Cain who?
Cain you come out and play?

Knock, knock.
Who's there?
Dewey.
Dewey who?
Dewey have to listen to all this knocking?

Knock, knock.
Who's there?
Candy.
Candy who?
Candy door be opened? I want to get out.

Duh...

Knock, knock.
Who's there?
Wooden shoe.
Wooden shoe who?
Wooden shoe like to know who's knocking at your
    door?

Knock, knock.
Who's there?
Winner.
Winner who?
Winner is when it snows.

Knock, knock.
Who's there?
I don't know. You haven't opened the door yet.

Knock, knock.
Who's there?
Taffilda.
Taffilda who?
Taffilda bucket you have to turn on the water.

Knock, knock.
Who's there?
Summertime.
Summertime who?
Summertime itsa hot, summertime itsa cold.

Knock, knock.
Who's there?
Stalin.
Stalin who?
Stalin for time!

Knock, knock.
Who's there?
Just a minute and I'll see.

Knock, knock.
Who's there?
I Sherwood.
I Sherwood who?
I Sherwood like to go home early from school
     today.

Knock, knock.
Who's there?
Paula.
Paula who?
Paula the handle; the door is open.

Knock, knock.
Who's there?
Odyssey.
Odyssey who?
Odyssey a dentist if your tooth hurts.

Knock, knock.
Who's there?
Nixon.
Nixon who?
Nixon stones will break my bones, but words will
never hurt me.

Knock, knock.
Who's there?
Nicholas.
Nicholas who?
Nicholas half as much as a dime.

Knock, knock.
Who's there?
Navajo.
Navajo who?
You'll Navajo until you open the door.

Knock, knock.
Who's there?
Morris.
Morris who?
Morris Saturday, next day's Sunday.

❖ ❖ ❖

Knock, knock.
Who's there?
Luke.
Luke who?
Luke who's there before you open the door.

❖ ❖ ❖

Knock, knock.
Who's there?
Lois.
Lois who?
Lois the opposite of high.

❖ ❖ ❖

Knock, knock.
Who's there?
Lionel.
Lionel who?
Lionel roar if you don't feed him.

❖ ❖ ❖

Knock, knock.
Who's there?
Kent.
Kent who?
Kent you see me?

❖ ❖ ❖

Knock, knock.
Who's there?
Karen.
Karen who?
Karen a load of bricks isn't much fun.

❖ ❖ ❖

Knock, knock.
Who's there?
Jacket.
Jacket who?
Jacket up if you've got a flat tire.

❖ ❖ ❖

Knock, knock.
Who's there?
Isadore.
Isadore who?
Isadore necessary?

❖ ❖ ❖

Knock, knock.
Who's there?
Iris.
Iris who?
Iris I was rich!

❖ ❖ ❖

Knock, knock.
Who's there?
Ira.
Ira who?
Ira-member you.

Knock, knock.
Who's there?
Imus.
Imus who?
Imus get out of this rain.

Knock, knock.
Who's there?
Howell.
Howell who?
Howell I get in if you don't open the door?

❖ ❖ ❖

Knock, knock.
Who's there?
Luke.
Luke who?
Luke both ways before crossing the street.

Knock, knock.
Who's there?
Hence.
Hence who?
Hence lay eggs.

Knock, knock.
Who's there?
Gladys.
Gladys who?
Gladys Friday—how 'bout you?

Knock, knock.
Who's there?
Eyewash.
Eyewash who?
Eyewash I had a million dollars.

Knock, knock.
Who's there?
Ellison.
Ellison who?
Ellison the alphabet after K.

❖ ❖ ❖

Knock, knock.
Who's there?
Doris.
Doris who?
Doris closed—that's why I knocked.

❖ ❖ ❖

Knock, knock.
Who's there?
Gladys.
Gladys who?
Gladys my last knock-knock joke?

❖ ❖ ❖

Knock, knock.
Who's there?
Denise.
Denise who?
Denise are connected to your legs.

❖ ❖ ❖

Knock, knock.
Who's there?
Chopin.
Chopin who?
Chopin the supermarket!

Knock, knock.
Who's there?
Cain.
Cain who?
Cain you hear me going knock knock?

❖ ❖ ❖

Knock, knock.
Who's there?
Cameron.
Cameron who?
Cameron film are what you need to take pictures.

❖ ❖ ❖

Knock, knock.
Who's there?
Doris.
Doris who?
Doris open. Mind if I come in?

❖ ❖ ❖

Knock, knock.
Who's there?
Attack.
Attack who?
Attack is sharp if you sit on it.

❖ ❖ ❖

Knock, knock.
Who's there?
Banana.
Banana who?

Knock, knock.
Who's there?
Banana.
Banana who?

Knock, knock.
Who's there?
Orange.
Orange who?
Orange you glad I didn't say "banana" again?

❖ ❖ ❖

Knock, knock.
Who's there?
Ahead.
Ahead who?
Ahead is on your shoulders.

❖ ❖ ❖

Knock, knock.
Who's there?
Allman.
Allman who?
Allman act silly.

Knock, knock.
Who's there?
Annie.
Annie who?
Annie-body home?

Knock, knock.
Who's there?
Arnold.
Arnold who?
Arnold you tired of all these knock-knock jokes?

Knock, knock.
Who's there?
Cargo.
Cargo who?
Cargo beep-beep.

Hey You!

Knock, knock.
Who's there?
Zoom.
Zoom who?
Zoom were you expecting?

❖ ❖ ❖

Knock, knock.
Who's there?
Yukon.
Yukon who?
Yukon let me in now.

❖ ❖ ❖

Knock, knock.
Who's there?
William Tell.
William Tell who?
William Tell your mother to come to the door.

Knock, knock.
Who's there?
Waiter.
Waiter who?
Waiter minute while I tie my shoe.

Knock, knock.
Who's there?
Usher.
Usher who?
Usher wish you would open the door.

Knock, knock.
Who's there?
Turner.
Turner who?
Turner handle and let me in!

Knock, knock.
Who's there?
Police.
Police who?
Police hurry up. It's chilly outside.

Knock, knock.
Who's there?
Phil.
Phil who?
Phil 'er up with regular, please.

Knock, knock.
Who's there?
Pepper.
Pepper who?
Pepper up. She looks tired.

Knock, knock.
Who's there?
Theodore.
Theodore who?
Theodore is closed, open up!

Knock, knock.
Who's there?
Milt.
Milt who?
Milt the cow.

Knock, knock.
Who's there?
Mikey.
Mikey who?
Mikey won't fit in this lock!

Knock, knock.
Who's there?
Martha.
Martha who?
Martha right over here and open the door!

Knock, knock.
Who's there?
Turner.
Turner who?
Turner round. I can't stand your face.

Knock, knock.
Who's there?
Major.
Major who?
Major open the door, didn't I!

Knock, knock.
Who's there?
Mack.
Mack who?
Mack up your mind.

Knock, knock.
Who's there?
Litter.
Litter who?
Litter go right now!

Knock, knock.
Who's there?
Leggo.
Leggo who?
Leggo the door—I wanna come in!

Knock, knock.
Who's there?
Kenya.
Kenya who?
Kenya hear me knocking?

Knock, knock.
Who's there?
Jewel.
Jewel who?
Jewel know when you open the door.

Knock, knock.
Who's there?
Jilly.
Jilly who?
Jilly out here, and I'm freezing. May I come in?

Knock, knock.
Who's there?
Ida.
Ida who?
Ida want to stand outside all night!

Knock, knock.
Who's there?
Hugh.
Hugh who?
Well, yoo-hoo to you, too!

Knock, knock.
Who's there?
Ida.
Ida who?
Ida 'ppreciate it if you'd open the door.

Knock, knock.
Who's there?
Police.
Police who?
Police open the door; it's raining out here.

Knock, knock.
Who's there?
Hominy.
Hominy who?
Hominy times do I have to knock at your door?

Knock, knock.
Who's there?
Heywood.
Heywood who?
Heywood you please open the door?

Knock, knock.
Who's there?
Harriet.
Harriet who?
Harriet up and open the door!

Knock, knock.
Who's there?
Handel.
Handel who?
Handel with care!

Knock, knock.
Who's there?
Sherwood.
Sherwood who?
Sherwood be nice if you opened the door.

Knock, knock.
Who's there?
Gary.
Gary who?
Gary me back to old Virginny…

Knock, knock.
Who's there?
Finish.
Finish who?
Finish it yourself!

Knock, knock.
Who's there?
Eva.
Eva who?
Eva since yesterday I've been knocking!

Knock, knock.
Who's there?
Enoch.
Enoch who?
Enoch and Enoch but nobody opens the door.

Knock, knock.
Who's there?
Donna.
Donna who?
Donna keep me waiting out here!

Knock, knock.
Who's there?
Dishes.
Dishes who?
Dishes me—open the door.

Knock, knock.
Who's there?
Colleen.
Colleen who?
Colleen up your room; it's a mess.

Knock, knock.
Who's there?
Colin.
Colin who?
Colin here and shut the door.

Knock, knock.
Who's there?
Ben.
Ben who?
Ben looking all over for you.

Knock, knock.
Who's there?
Chuck.
Chuck who?
Chuck and see if the door is unlocked.

Knock, knock.
Who's there?
Chaise.
Chaise who?
Chaised him away.

Knock, knock.
Who's there?
Censure.
Censure who?
Censure so smart, why aren't you rich?

Knock, knock.
Who's there?
Celeste.
Celeste who?
Celeste time I'll ask you.

Knock, knock.
Who's there?
Carla.
Carla who?
Carla locksmith. My key won't work.

Knock, knock.
Who's there?
Carrie.
Carrie who?
Carrie me inside—I'm tired.

Knock, knock.
Who's there?
Butter.
Butter who?
Butter be home before midnight.

Knock, knock.
Who's there?
Butcher.
Butcher who?
Butcher feet on the floor.

Knock, knock.
Who's there?
Ben.
Ben who?
Ben down and tie my shoes, please.

Knock, knock.
Who's there?
Atlas.
Atlas who?
Atlas you answered the door!

Knock, knock.
Who's there?
Carrie.
Carrie who?
Carrie me back to bed. I'm tired.

Knock, knock.
Who's there?
Adore.
Adore who?
Adore is between us. Open up.

Knock, knock.
Who's there?
Apricot.
Apricot who?
Apricot my key. Open up!

Knock, knock.
Who's there?
Abbot.
Abbot who?
Abbot time you answered the door.

Knock, knock.
Who's there?
Boo.
Boo who?
Crybaby!

Huh?

Knock, knock.
Who's there?
Boop-boop.
Boop-boop who?
Boop-boop-de-doo.

❖ ❖ ❖

Knock, knock.
Who's there?
Tara.
Tara who?
Tara-ra-boom-de-ay!

❖ ❖ ❖

Knock, knock.
Who's there?
Zippy.
Zippy who?
Mrs. Zippy. Can you spell that without any i's?

Knock, knock.
Who's there?
Dozen.
Dozen who?
Dozen anyone want to let me in?

Knock, knock.
Who's there?
Dill.
Dill who?
Big Dill.

Knock, knock.
Who's there?
Yul.
Yul who?
Yul never know without opening the door!

Knock, knock.
Who's there?
Wire.
Wire who?
Wire we telling knock-knock jokes?

Knock, knock.
Who's there?
Who Who.
Who Who who?
You sound like an owl.

Knock, knock.
Who's there?
Wendy.
Wendy who?
Wendy wind blows, the cradle will rock...

Knock, knock.
Who's there?
Turnip.
Turnip who?
Turnip the TV.

Knock, knock.
Who's there?
Toodle.
Toodle who?
Toodle who to you, too!

❖ ❖ ❖

Knock, knock.
Who's there?
Sultan.
Sultan who?
Sultan pepper.

❖ ❖ ❖

Knock, knock.
Who's there?
Sarah.
Sarah who?
Sarah echo in here?

❖ ❖ ❖

Knock, knock.
Who's there?
Pressure.
Pressure who?
Pressure shirt?

❖ ❖ ❖

Knock, knock.
Who's there?
Peeper.
Peeper who?
Peeper and salt, that's who.

Knock, knock.
Who's there?
Olga.
Olga who?
Olga 'round to the back door.

Knock, knock.
Who's there?
Norma Lee.
Norma Lee who?
Norma Lee I don't ring other people's doorbells.

Knock, knock.
Who's there?
Mush.
Mush who?
Mush be 20 past 8.

Knock, knock.
Who's there?
Missy.
Missy who?
Missy-laneous.

Knock, knock.
Who's there?
Kleenex.
Kleenex who?
Kleenex are prettier than dirty necks.

Knock, knock.
Who's there?
Turnip.
Turnip who?
Turnip your pants at the bottom—they're too long.

Knock, knock.
Who's there?
Ben Hur.
Ben Hur who?
Ben Hur waiting ten minutes.

Knock, knock.
Who's there?
Juneau.
Juneau who?
No, I don't. Do you?

❖ ❖ ❖

Knock, knock.
Who's there?
Juan.
Juan who?
Juan, two, buckle my shoe.

❖ ❖ ❖

Knock, knock.
Who's there?
Idaho.
Idaho who?
Idaho my own name.

❖ ❖ ❖

Knock, knock.
Who's there?
Hugh.
Hugh who?
Hugh-mility.

❖ ❖ ❖

Knock, knock.
Who's there?
Franz.
Franz who?
Franz…Romans…countrymen…lend me your ears.

Knock, knock.
Who's there?
Deep.
Deep who?
Deep-ends on who you were expecting.

Knock, knock.
Who's there?
Costa.
Costa who?
Costa lot.

Knock, knock.
Who's there?
Abbot.
Abbot who?
Abbot you don't know who this is!

Knock, knock.
Who's there?
Amnesia.
Amnesia who?
Oh, I see you have it, too!

Knock, knock.
Who's there?
Ben Hur.
Ben Hur who?
Ben Hur an hour and no one has opened the door.

Knock, knock.
Who's there?
A little boy who can't reach the doorbell.

It's the Truth

Knock, knock.
Who's there?
Unawares.
Unawares who?
Unawares what you put on first every morning.

Knock, knock.
Who's there?
Arthur.
Arthur who?
Arthur-mometer is broken.

Knock, knock.
Who's there?
Ben.
Ben who?
Ben walkin' the dog.

Knock, knock.
Who's there?
Zeke.
Zeke who?
Zeke and you shall find; knock and the door shall
    be opened.

Knock, knock.
Who's there?
Yuri.
Yuri who?
Yuri great person.

Knock, knock.
Who's there?
Whittier.
Whittier who?
Whittier people always tell knock-knock jokes!

Knock, knock.
Who's there?
Uriah.
Uriah who?
Keep Uriah on the peep hole and you can see who
is knocking.

Knock, knock.
Who's there?
Toucan.
Toucan who?
Toucan live as cheaply as one.

Knock, knock.
Who's there?
Sherwood.
Sherwood who?
Sherwood like to eat dinner with you.

Knock, knock.
Who's there?
Sanctuary.
Sanctuary who?
Sanctuary much!

Knock, knock.
Who's there?
Rubber duck.
Rubber duck who?
Rubber duck dub…three men in a tub…

Knock, knock.
Who's there?
Ripsaw.
Ripsaw who?
Ripsaw you downtown yesterday.

Knock, knock.
Who's there?
Rhoda.
Rhoda who?
Rhoda horse back after crossing the lake.

Knock, knock.
Who's there?
Phyllis.
Phyllis who?
Phyllis on the news.

Knock, knock.
Who's there?
Opera.
Opera who?
Opera-tunity.

Knock, knock.
Who's there?
Opera.
Opera who?
Opera-tunity always knocks more than once.

Knock, knock.
Who's there?
Oliver.
Oliver who?
Oliver troubles will soon be over.

Knock, knock.
Who's there?
Mayonnaise.
Mayonnaise who?
Mayonnaise have seen the glory of the coming of
the Lord...

Knock, knock.
Who's there?
Mabel.
Mabel who?
Mabel I'll tell you, and Mabel I won't.

❖ ❖ ❖

Knock, knock.
Who's there?
Huron.
Huron who?
Huron time for once.

❖ ❖ ❖

Knock, knock.
Who's there?
Hosea.
Hosea who?
Hosea can you see?

❖ ❖ ❖

Knock, knock.
Who's there?
Gibbon.
Gibbon who?
Gibbon take is a good way to share.

❖ ❖ ❖

Knock, knock.
Who's there?
Fido.
Fido who?
Fido known you were coming, I would have baked
a cake.

Knock, knock.
Who's there?
Eskimo, Christian, Italian.
Eskimo, Christian, Italian who?
Eskimo, Christian, Italian no lies.

Knock, knock.
Who's there?
Distress.
Distress who?
Distress is very short.

Knock, knock.
Who's there?
Dishwasher.
Dishwasher who?
Dishwashern't the way I shpoke before I had falsh
teeth.

Knock, knock.
Who's there?
Cantaloupe.
Cantaloupe who?
Cantaloupe without a ladder.

Knock, knock.
Who's there?
A cheetah.
A cheetah who?
A cheetah never wins.

Just the Facts

Knock, knock.
Who's there?
Eileen.
Eileen who?
Eileen over to tie my shoes.

Knock, knock.
Who's there?
Zombies.
Zombies who?
Zombies make honey, and zombies just buzz
    around.

Knock, knock.
Who's there?
Weed.
Weed who?
Weed better mow the lawn before it gets too long.

Knock, knock.
Who's there?
Walter.
Walter who?
Walter-wall carpeting for sale. Would you like some?

Knock, knock.
Who's there?
Tomb.
Tomb who?
Tomb it may concern…

Knock, knock.
Who's there?
Tamara.
Tamara who?
Tamara it's gonna rain.

Knock, knock.
Who's there?
Swarm.
Swarm who?
Swarm enough to go swimming.

Knock, knock.
Who's there?
Sofa.
Sofa who?
Sofa you're doing fine.

Knock, knock.
Who's there?
Scold.
Scold who?
Scold enough to go ice-skating.

Knock, knock.
Who's there?
Salmon.
Salmon who?
Salmon Jack are over at my house.

Knock, knock.
Who's there?
Roxanne.
Roxanne who?
Roxanne shells were on the beach.

Knock, knock.
Who's there?
Rhoda.
Rhoda who?
Rhoda boat across the lake.

Knock, knock.
Who's there?
Phillip.
Phillip who?
Phillip the tank—I'm out of gas!

Knock, knock.
Who's there?
Ocelot.
Ocelot who?
Ocelot of questions for a doorkeeper.

Knock, knock.
Who's there?
Lion.
Lion who?
Lion down on the job, eh?

Knock, knock.
Who's there?
Ivan.
Ivan who?
Ivan working on the railroad, all the live-long day...

Knock, knock.
Who's there?
Iona.
Iona who?
Iona new car.

Knock, knock.
Who's there?
Iowa.
Iowa who?
Iowa dollar.

❖ ❖ ❖

Knock, knock.
Who's there?
Ice cream.
Ice cream who?
Ice cream 'cause I'm a cheerleader.

Knock, knock.
Who's there?
Hank.
Hank who?
Hank E. Chief.

Knock, knock.
Who's there?
Esau.
Esau who?
Esau him looking out the window.

Knock, knock.
Who's there?
Emma.
Emma who?
Emma tired. Are you tired, too?

Knock, knock.
Who's there?
Eclipse.
Eclipse who?
Eclipse my hair in the barbershop.

Knock, knock.
Who's there?
Dwayne.
Dwayne who?
Dwayne in Spain falls mainly on da plain.

Knock, knock.
Who's there?
Despair.
Despair who?
Despair tire is flat.

Knock, knock.
Who's there?
China.
China who?
China cold out, isn't it?

Knock, knock.
Who's there?
Choo-choo train.
Choo-choo train who?
Choo-choo trained the lion, but the tiger wouldn't
    cooperate.

Knock, knock.
Who's there?
Cecil.
Cecil who?
Cecil have music wherever she goes.

Knock, knock.
Who's there?
Cartoon.
Cartoon who?
Cartoon-ups are necessary to keep your car running
    smoothly.

Let's Party!

Knock, knock.
Who's there?
Ya.
Ya who?
I'm glad you're having fun!

❖ ❖ ❖

Knock, knock.
Who's there?
Waterloo.
Waterloo who?
Waterloo doing for dinner?

❖ ❖ ❖

Knock, knock.
Who's there?
Wanda.
Wanda who?
Wanda come out and play?

Knock, knock.
Who's there?
Vicious.
Vicious who?
Vicious a merry Christmas!

Knock, knock.
Who's there?
Venice.
Venice who?
Venice your next birthday?

Knock, knock.
Who's there?
Tuna.
Tuna who?
Tuna to a rock station!

Knock, knock.
Who's there?
Sue.
Sue who?
Sue Prize!

Knock, knock.
Who's there?
Shirley.
Shirley who?
Shirley you're going to open the door.

Knock, knock.
Who's there?
Sandy.
Sandy who?
Sandy Claus!

Knock, knock.
Who's there?
Samoa.
Samoa who?
Samoa'l friends from school.

Knock, knock.
Who's there?
Phyllis.
Phyllis who?
Phyllis glass up with soda, please. I'm thirsty.

Knock, knock.
Who's there?
Norma Lee.
Norma Lee who?
Norma Lee we go swimming on Sundays, but we
    thought we'd visit you instead.

Knock, knock.
Who's there?
Mountie.
Mountie who?
Mountie horses and go for a ride.

Knock, knock.
Who's there?
Mark.
Mark who?
Mark the herald angels sing...

❖ ❖ ❖

Knock, knock.
Who's there?
Louis.
Louis who?
Louis'n up!

❖ ❖ ❖

Knock, knock.
Who's there?
Justice.
Justice who?
Justice I thought. No one's home.

❖ ❖ ❖

Knock, knock.
Who's there?
Irish.
Irish who?
Irish you a merry Christmas!

❖ ❖ ❖

Knock, knock.
Who's there?
Iran.
Iran who?
Iran over to see you.

❖ ❖ ❖

Knock, knock.
Who's there?
Hume.
Hume who?
Hume did you expect?

❖ ❖ ❖

Knock, knock.
Who's there?
Hugh.
Hugh who?
Hugh better watch out, Hugh better not cry.

❖ ❖ ❖

Knock, knock.
Who's there?
Howie.
Howie who?
Fine, thanks. Howie you?

❖ ❖ ❖

Knock, knock.
Who's there?
Hollywood.
Hollywood who?
Hollywood be here if she could!

❖ ❖ ❖

Knock, knock.
Who's there?
A herd.
A herd who?
A herd you were home, so I came over!

❖ ❖ ❖

Knock, knock.
Who's there?
Havana.
Havana who?
Havana good time.

❖ ❖ ❖

Knock, knock.
Who's there?
Heaven.
Heaven who?
Heaven seen you for a long, long time.

❖ ❖ ❖

Knock, knock.
Who's there?
Happy.
Happy who?
Happy birthday to you!

❖ ❖ ❖

Knock, knock.
Who's there?
Hank.
Hank who?
Hank you for opening the door.

❖ ❖ ❖

Knock, knock.
Who's there?
Gladys.
Gladys who?
Gladys see you.

❖ ❖ ❖

Knock, knock.
Who's there?
Freddie.
Freddie who?
Freddie or not...here I come!

❖ ❖ ❖

Knock, knock.
Who's there?
Freeze.
Freeze who?
Freeze a jolly good fellow...

Knock, knock.
Who's there?
Fresno.
Fresno who?
Rudolf the Fresno Reindeer.

Knock, knock.
Who's there?
Ford.
Ford who?
Ford he's a jolly good fellow...

Knock, knock.
Who's there?
Fitzby.
Fitzby who?
Fitzby-ginning to look a lot like Christmas...

Knock, knock.
Who's there?
Farley.
Farley who?
Farley the leader.

Knock, knock.
Who's there?
Easter.
Easter who?
Easter anybody home?

Knock, knock.
Who's there?
Dynamite.
Dynamite who?
Dynamite play with us if we're good.

Knock, knock.
Who's there?
Duke.
Duke who?
Duke the halls with boughs of holly...

Knock, knock.
Who's there?
Celia.
Celia who?
Celia later.

❖ ❖ ❖

Knock, knock.
Who's there?
Celeste.
Celeste who?
Celeste time I'll tell you a knock-knock joke.

❖ ❖ ❖

Knock, knock.
Who's there?
Cargo.
Cargo who?
Cargo beep-beep and ran over the Easter bunny.

❖ ❖ ❖

Knock, knock.
Who's there?
Boo.
Boo who?
Don't cry. Easter bunny be back next year.

❖ ❖ ❖

Knock, knock.
Who's there?
Caesar.
Caesar who?
Caesar jolly good fellow, Caesar jolly good fellow...

Knock, knock.
Who's there?
Abbey.
Abbey who?
Abbey birthday.

Knock, knock.
Who's there?
Altoona.
Altoona who?
Altoona piano and you play it.

Lovesick

Knock, knock.
Who's there?
Yura.
Yura who?
Yura great friend.

❖ ❖ ❖

Knock, knock.
Who's there?
Wooden.
Wooden who?
Wooden you like to go out with me?

❖ ❖ ❖

Knock, knock.
Who's there?
Witless.
Witless who?
Witless ring I thee wed.

Knock, knock.
Who's there?
Wilfred.
Wilfred who?
Wilfred call me tonight?

Knock, knock.
Who's there?
Warrior.
Warrior who?
Warrior been all my life?

Knock, knock.
Who's there?
Value.
Value who?
Value be my valentine?

Knock, knock.
Who's there?
Soda.
Soda who?
Soda you like me?

Knock, knock.
Who's there?
Sherwood.
Sherwood who?
Sherwood like it if you'd let me kiss you.

Knock, knock.
Who's there?
Sam.
Sam who?
Sam-day my prince will come.

Knock, knock.
Who's there?
Owl.
Owl who?
Owl never tell.

Knock, knock.
Who's there?
Olive.
Olive who?
Olive who, too, honey.

Knock, knock.
Who's there?
Navajo.
Navajo who?
You'll Navajo just how much I miss you.

Knock, knock.
Who's there?
Myth.
Myth who?
I myth you, too.

Knock, knock.
Who's there?
Sam and Janet.
Sam and Janet who?
Sam and Janet evening, you will meet a good-
    looking stranger.

Knock, knock.
Who's there?
Mecca.
Mecca who?
Mecca me happy!

Knock, knock.
Who's there?
Kay.
Kay who?
Kay sera sera.

Knock, knock.
Who's there?
Willa.
Willa who?
Willa you go on a date with me?

Knock, knock.
Who's there?
Oscar.
Oscar who?
Oscar if she loves me.

❖ ❖ ❖

Knock, knock.
Who's there?
Ivan.
Ivan who?
Ivan wanting to hold your hand.

❖ ❖ ❖

Knock, knock.
Who's there?
Israeli.
Israeli who?
Israeli great to see you again.

❖ ❖ ❖

Knock, knock.
Who's there?
Iguana.
Iguana who?
Iguana hold your hand.

❖ ❖ ❖

Knock, knock.
Who's there?
Hugo.
Hugo who?
Wherever hugo, I go, too.

❖ ❖ ❖

Knock, knock.
Who's there?
Howard.
Howard who?
Howard you like to be my valentine?

❖ ❖ ❖

Knock, knock.
Who's there?
Honeydew.
Honeydew who?
Honeydew you love me?

❖ ❖ ❖

Knock, knock.
Who's there?
Cantaloupe.
Cantaloupe who?
Honey, I love you, but we cantaloupe now.

❖ ❖ ❖

Knock, knock.
Who's there?
Hair combs.
Hair combs who?
Hair combs the bride!

❖ ❖ ❖

Knock, knock.
Who's there?
Halibut.
Halibut who?
Halibut a kiss, sweetie?

❖ ❖ ❖

Knock, knock.
Who's there?
Ivan.
Ivan who?
Ivan wanting to drop over.

❖ ❖ ❖

Knock, knock.
Who's there?
Ghana.
Ghana who?
Ghana wash that man right out of my hair...

❖ ❖ ❖

Knock, knock.
Who's there?
Ferry.
Ferry who?
Ferry-tales can come true.

Knock, knock.
Who's there?
Elsie.
Elsie who?
Elsie you in my dreams.

Knock, knock.
Who's there?
Emerson.
Emerson who?
Emerson big eyes you've got, baby.

Knock, knock.
Who's there?
Elder.
Elder who?
Elder in my arms all evening.

Knock, knock.
Who's there?
Just Diane.
Just Diane who?
Just Diane to see you.

❖ ❖ ❖

Knock, knock.
Who's there?
Deboy.
Deboy who?
Deboy is cute.

❖ ❖ ❖

Knock, knock.
Who's there?
Cash.
Cash who?
Cash me if you can!

❖ ❖ ❖

Knock, knock.
Who's there?
Bwana.
Bwana who?
Bwana hold your hand.

❖ ❖ ❖

Knock, knock.
Who's there?
Butcher.
Butcher who?
Butcher arms around me and hold me tight.

Knock, knock.
Who's there?
Butch, Jimmy, and Joe.
Butch, Jimmy, and Joe who?
Butch your arms around me, Jimmy a kiss, or I'll
    Joe home.

Knock, knock.
Who's there?
Be.
Be who?
Be down to get you in a taxi, honey.

Knock, knock.
Who's there?
Bay.
Bay who?
Baybeface, you've got the cutest little baby face!

Knock, knock.
Who's there?
Aster.
Aster who?
Aster yourself.

❖ ❖ ❖

Knock, knock.
Who's there?
Althea.
Althea who?
Althea in my dreams.

❖ ❖ ❖

Knock, knock.
Who's there?
Apollo.
Apollo who?
Apollo you anywhere if you'll give me a kiss.

❖ ❖ ❖

Knock, knock.
Who's there?
Aster.
Aster who?
Aster if she kept a diary.

Mmmm—Tasty!

Knock, knock.
Who's there?
Lettuce.
Lettuce who?
Lettuce pray.

❖ ❖ ❖

Knock, knock.
Who's there?
Cereal.
Cereal who?
Cereal soon.

❖ ❖ ❖

Knock, knock.
Who's there?
Carmen.
Carmen who?
Carmen get it.

Knock, knock.
Who's there?
Sweden.
Sweden who?
Sweden my tea with two lumps of sugar.

Knock, knock.
Who's there?
C-I-A.
C-I-A who?
C-I-Ate the whole cake!

Knock, knock.
Who's there?
Willie.
Willie who?
Willie be home for dinner?

Knock, knock.
Who's there?
Roland.
Roland who?
Roland butter sure taste good.

Knock, knock.
Who's there?
Red.
Red who?
Red pepper. Isn't that a hot one?

Knock, knock.
Who's there?
Possum.
Possum who?
Possum ketchup for my hamburger.

Knock, knock.
Who's there?
Phyllis.
Phyllis who?
Phyllis pitcher with water, please.

Knock, knock.
Who's there?
Passion.
Passion who?
Passion by and I thought I'd see what's for dinner.

Knock, knock.
Who's there?
Pasta.
Pasta who?
Pasta pizza—I'm starved.

Knock, knock.
Who's there?
Marsha.
Marsha who?
Marsha Mallow.

Knock, knock.
Who's there?
Manila.
Manila who?
Manila ice cream!

Knock, knock.
Who's there?
Lemon Juice.
Lemon Juice who?
Lemon Juice you to my friend.

Knock, knock.
Who's there?
Ketchup.
Ketchup who?
Ketchup to her before she turns the corner.

Knock, knock.
Who's there?
Henrietta.
Henrietta who?
Henrietta worm that was in his apple

Knock, knock.
Who's there?
Hamen.
Hamen who?
Hamen eggs.

Knock, knock.
Who's there?
Doughnut.
Doughnut who?
Doughnut open until Christmas.

Knock, knock.
Who's there?
Frank.
Frank who?
Frank and beans.

Knock, knock.
Who's there?
Frankfurter.
Frankfurter who?
Frankfurter memories.

Knock, knock.
Who's there?
Duncan.
Duncan who?
Duncan doughnuts in your milk makes 'em soft.

Knock, knock.
Who's there?
Catsup.
Catsup who?
Catsup a tree. Call the fire department!

Knock, knock.
Who's there?
Carfare.
Carfare who?
Carfare a cookie or a piece of cake?

Knock, knock.
Who's there?
Beckon.
Beckon who?
Beckon goes well with eggs.

Knock, knock.
Who's there?
Barbie.
Barbie who?
Barbie Q Chicken.

Knock, knock.
Who's there?
Ketchup.
Ketchup who?
Ketchup with me, and I'll tell you a secret.

Knock, knock.
Who's there?
Aida.
Aida who?
Aida sandwich at recess time.

Ouch!

Knock, knock.
Who's there?
Eiffel.
Eiffel who?
Eiffel down and broke my crown.

❖   ❖   ❖

Knock, knock.
Who's there?
Andrew.
Andrew who?
Andrew a picture of me today.

❖   ❖   ❖

Knock, knock.
Who's there?
My Tommy.
My Tommy who?
My Tommy aches.

Knock, knock.
Who's there?
Tacoma.
Tacoma who?
Tacoma all this way and you don't recognize me!

Knock, knock.
Who's there?
Spinach.
Spinach who?
Spinaching so long I had to scratch it.

Knock, knock.
Who's there?
Shad.
Shad who?
Shad up and open the door.

Knock, knock.
Who's there?
Senior.
Senior who?
Senior so nosy, I won't tell you.

Knock, knock.
Who's there?
Sara.
Sara who?
Sara doctor in the house? These jokes are sick.

Knock, knock.
Who's there?
Pasture.
Pasture who?
Pasture bedtime. You need your beauty sleep.

Knock, knock.
Who's there?
Oswald.
Oswald who?
Oswald mah gum.

Knock, knock.
Who's there?
Orange.
Orange who?
Orange you ever coming home?

Knock, knock.
Who's there?
Oliver.
Oliver who?
Oliver my body the mosquitoes are biting me.

Knock, knock.
Who's there?
Nunna.
Nunna who?
Nunna your business.

Knock, knock.
Who's there?
Minervas.
Minervas who?
Minervas a wreck from all these sick jokes.

Knock, knock.
Who's there?
Mariet.
Mariet who?
Mariet the whole bowl of popcorn.

Knock, knock.
Who's there?
Sarah.
Sarah who?
Sarah doctor that can stop all this itching?

Knock, knock.
Who's there?
Mandy.
Mandy who?
Mandy lifeboats. I'm drowning.

Knock, knock.
Who's there?
Lion.
Lion who?
Lion can sure get you in trouble.

Knock, knock.
Who's there?
Juan.
Juan who?
Juan to hear some more knock-knock jokes?

Knock, knock.
Who's there?
Ivor.
Ivor who?
Ivor sore hand from knocking on this door.

Knock, knock.
Who's there?
Ivan.
Ivan who?
Ivan itch and I can't reach it. Will you scratch it for
    me?

Knock, knock.
Who's there?
Isaac.
Isaac who?
Isaac. Call a doctor.

Knock, knock.
Who's there?
Formosa.
Formosa who?
Formosa the day I was in the principal's office.

Knock, knock.
Who's there?
Doughnut.
Doughnut who?
Doughnut close the door, my foot is in it.

Knock, knock.
Who's there?
Ferdie.
Ferdie who?
Ferdie last time, will you please open the door? My
    foot is still in it.

Knock, knock.
Who's there?
Canoe.
Canoe who?
Canoe please get off my foot?

Knock, knock.
Who's there?
Duane.
Duane who?
Duane the tub—I'm drowning!

Knock, knock.
Who's there?
Despair.
Despair who?
Despair of shoes is too tight.

Knock, knock.
Who's there?
Congo.
Congo who?
Congo out, I'm grounded.

Knock, knock.
Who's there?
Avenue.
Avenue who?
Avenue heard the good news? I've got more knock-
    knock jokes!

❖ ❖ ❖

Knock, knock.
Who's there?
Formosa.
Formosa who?
Formosa the term I was absent from school.

Knock, knock.
Who's there?
Adolf.
Adolf who?
Adolf ball hit me in the mowf.

❖ ❖ ❖

Knock, knock.
Who's there?
Agatha.
Agatha who?
Agatha headache. Do you have any aspirin?

❖ ❖ ❖

Knock, knock.
Who's there?
Aida.
Aida who?
Aida lot of ice cream and my stomach hurts.

You Don't Say...

Knock, knock.
Who's there?
Yah.
Yah who?
Gosh, I'm glad to see you too!

Knock, knock.
Who's there?
Ella.
Ella who?
Ella-vator. Doesn't that give you a lift?

Knock, knock.
Who's there?
Gus.
Gus who?
Gus who's coming to dinner?

Knock, knock.
Who's there?
Ghana.
Ghana who?
Ghana make you laugh!

Knock, knock.
Who's there?
Heel.
Heel who?
Heel be right back.

Knock, knock.
Who's there?
Santa Ana.
Santa Ana who?
Santa Ana gonna bring you anything if you don't
    believe in him.

Knock, knock.
Who's there?
Eisenhower
Eisenhower who?
Eisenhower late for work.

❖ ❖ ❖

Knock, knock.
Who's there?
Wendy.
Wendy who?
Wendy door opens, I'll come in.

❖ ❖ ❖

Knock, knock.
Who's there?
Weevil.
Weevil who?
Weevil see you later.

❖ ❖ ❖

Knock, knock.
Who's there?
Thistle.
Thistle who?
Thistle make you whistle.

❖ ❖ ❖

Knock, knock.
Who's there?
Summertime.
Summertime who?
Summertime I'm going to stop telling knock-knock
   jokes.

Knock, knock.
Who's there?
Roach.
Roach who?
Roach you a letter—did you get it?

Knock, knock.
Who's there?
Orange juice.
Orange juice who?
Orange juice sorry you made me cry?

Knock, knock.
Who's there?
Ireland.
Ireland who?
Ireland you a quarter if you promise to pay me back.

❖ ❖ ❖

Knock, knock.
Who's there?
Alfred.
Alfred who?
Alfred the needle if you'll sew the button on.

❖ ❖ ❖

Knock, knock.
Who's there?
Alex.
Alex who?
Alex-plain later.

❖ ❖ ❖

Knock, knock.
Who's there?
Akron.
Akron who?
Akron give you anything but love, baby.

❖ ❖ ❖

Knock, knock.
Who's there?
Alaska.
Alaska who?
Alaska no questions; you tella no lies.

P-U

Knock, knock.
Who's there?
Aaron.
Aaron who?
Aaron out my stinky gym locker.

Knock, knock.
Who's there?
Isle.
Isle who?
Isle give you a big kiss if you open the door.

Knock, knock.
Who's there?
Robin.
Robin who?
Robin a coffin is dangerous. You could be in grave
trouble.

Knock, knock.
Who's there?
Phillip.
Phillip who?
Phillip the tub so I can take a bath.

Knock, knock.
Who's there?
Cayuse.
Cayuse who?
Cayuse your bathroom?

Knock, knock.
Who's there?
Butternut.
Butternut who?
Butternut try to pick up a skunk.

❖ ❖ ❖

Knock, knock.
Who's there?
Samoa.
Samoa who?
Samoa knock-knock jokes.

❖ ❖ ❖

Knock, knock.
Who's there?
Anita.
Anita who?
Anita take a bath.

❖ ❖ ❖

Knock, knock.
Who's there?
April.
April who?
April showers.

Quit That!

Knock, knock.
Who's there?
Wayne.
Wayne who?
Wayne, Wayne, go away, come again another day.

❖ ❖ ❖

Knock, knock.
Who's there?
York.
York who?
York, york, york. This is funny.

Knock, knock.
Who's there?
Boo-hoo.
Boo-hoo who?
Boo-hoo-hoo.
Boo-hoo-hoo who?
Boo-hoo-hoo-hoo.
Boo-hoo-hoo-hoo who?
Boo-hoo-hoo-hoo-hoo.
Boo-hoo-hoo-hoo-hoo who?
Stop it! You're breaking my heart.

Knock, knock.
Who's there?
Closure.
Closure who?
Closure mouth, I'm talking!

Knock, knock.
Who's there?
Cook.
Cook who?
Cut the bird impressions, I want to come in!

Knock, knock.
Who's there?
Hans.
Hans who?
Hans off the table!

Knock, knock.
Who's there?
Soda lady.
Soda lady who?
Quit yodeling and get back to work!

Knock, knock.
Who's there?
Anita.
Anita who?
Anita minute to think it over.

Knock, knock.
Who's there?
Yoda.
Yoda who?
Yoda le-hee-who!

Knock, knock.
Who's there?
William.
William who?
Williamind your own business!

Knock, knock.
Who's there?
Water.
Water who?
Water you doing?

Knock, knock.
Who's there?
Uganda.
Uganda who?
Uganda ask me to come in?

Knock, knock.
Who's there?
Police.
Police who?
Police stop telling knock-knock jokes!

Knock, knock.
Who's there?
Pecan.
Pecan who?
Pecan somebody your own size.

Knock, knock.
Who's there?
Nana.
Nana who?
Nana your business.

Knock, knock.
Who's there?
Major.
Major who?
Major ask, didn't I?

Knock, knock.
Who's there?
Lyndon.
Lyndon who?
Lyndon me an ear, and I'll tell you another knock-
    knock joke.

Knock, knock.
Who's there?
Doughnut.
Doughnut who?
Doughnut bother me with silly questions!

Knock, knock.
Who's there?
Tallotta.
Tallotta who?
Tallotta noise you're making.

Knock, knock.
Who's there?
Celeste.
Celeste who?
Celeste time I knock on this door!

What's That?

Knock, knock.
Who's there?
Zing.
Zing who?
Zing like a bird!

❖ ❖ ❖

Knock, knock.
Who's there?
You.
You who?
Who are you calling?

❖ ❖ ❖

Knock, knock.
Who's there?
Who.
Who who?
There's a terrible echo in here, isn't there?

Knock, knock.
Who's there?
Violet.
Violet who?
Violet you make these jokes, I'll never understand.

Knock, knock.
Who's there?
Wednesday.
Wednesday who?
Wednesday saints go marching in…

Knock, knock.
Who's there?
Water.
Water who?
Water you know?

Knock, knock.
Who's there?
Tuba.
Tuba who?
Tuba toothpaste.

❖ ❖ ❖

Knock, knock.
Who's there?
Tick.
Tick who?
Tick 'em up.

❖ ❖ ❖

Knock, knock.
Who's there?
Telly.
Telly who?
Telly-phone.

❖ ❖ ❖

Knock, knock.
Who's there?
Summons.
Summons who?
Summons at the door knocking.

❖ ❖ ❖

Knock, knock.
Who's there?
Socket.
Socket who?
Socket to me!

Knock, knock.
Who's there?
Sacha.
Sacha who?
Sacha fuss just because I knocked on your door.

Knock, knock.
Who's there?
Rita.
Rita who?
Rita good book lately?

Knock, knock.
Who's there?
Perry.
Perry who?
Perry-scope.

Knock, knock.
Who's there?
Pasture.
Pasture who?
Pasture test, didn't you?

Knock, knock.
Who's there?
Orange.
Orange who?
Orange you glad I'm here?

Knock knock.
Who's there?
Annette.
Annette who?
Annette is what you need to play tennis.

Knock, knock.
Who's there?
Norma Lee.
Norma Lee who?
Norma Lee I don't talk to strangers.

Knock, knock.
Who's there?
Nobody.
Nobody who?
Nobody. I'm just banging on the door.

Knock, knock.
Who's there?
Noah.
Noah who?
Noah good knock-knock joke?

Knock, knock.
Who's there?
Newton.
Newton who?
Newton doing.

Knock, knock.
Who's there?
Moscow.
Moscow who?
Moscow gives more milk than pa's cow.

Knock, knock.
Who's there?
Monopoly.
Monopoly who?
Monopoly's bigger than your nopoly.

Knock, knock.
Who's there?
Mecca.
Mecca who?
Mecca noise like a duck.

Knock, knock.
Who's there?
Little old lady.
Little old lady who?
I didn't know you could yodel!

Knock, knock.
Who's there?
Lettuce.
Lettuce who?
Lettuce go see a movie.

Knock, knock.
Who's there?
Justin.
Justin who?
Justin time for supper.

Knock, knock.
Who's there?
Joint.
Joint who?
Joint you know who is knocking?

Knock, knock.
Who's there?
Ivy League.
Ivy League who?
Ivy League for every drop of rain that falls, a flower
   grows.

Knock, knock.
Who's there?
Iben.
Iben who?
Iben a good boy.

Knock, knock.
Who's there?
Annapolis.
Annapolis who?
Annapolis a fruit.

Knock, knock.
Who's there?
Annette.
Annette who?
Annette is needed to catch butterflies.

Where?

Knock, knock.
Who's there?
Oscar.
Oscar who?
Oscar if she wants to go to the party.

Knock, knock.
Who's there?
Divan.
Divan who?
Divan the pool and go swimming.

❖ ❖ ❖

Knock, knock.
Who's there?
Howl.
Howl who?
Howl it be if I come to your house today?

Knock, knock.
Who's there?
Wren.
Wren who?
Wren are you coming out?

Knock, knock.
Who's there?
Carmen.
Carmen who?
"Carmen to my parlor," said the spider to the fly.

Knock, knock.
Who's there?
Kenya.
Kenya who?
Kenya open the door?

Knock, knock.
Who's there?
Pocket.
Pocket who?
Pocket in the pocking lot.

Knock, knock.
Who's there?
Domino.
Domino who?
Domino cowhand…from the Rio Grande…

Knock, knock.
Who's there?
Weirdo.
Weirdo who?
Weirdo the deer and the antelope play?

Knock, knock.
Who's there?
Warrant.
Warrant who?
Warrant you home before?

Knock, knock.
Who's there?
Somber.
Somber who?
Somber over the rainbow...

Knock, knock.
Who's there?
Rocky.
Rocky who?
Rocky bye baby in the treetop...

Knock, knock.
Who's there?
Osborn.
Osborn who?
Osborn down in Mississippi. Where were you born?

Knock, knock.
Who's there?
Moth.
Moth who?
Moth grows on the north side of trees.

Knock, knock.
Who's there?
Lily.
Lily who?
Lily house on the prairie.

Knock, knock.
Who's there?
Kangar.
Kangar who?
Kangar whos live in Australia.

Knock, knock.
Who's there?
Utah Nevada.
Utah Nevada who?
Utah Nevada guess where I went for a vacation.

Knock, knock.
Who's there?
Jupiter.
Jupiter who?
Jupiter fly in my soup?

Knock, knock.
Who's there?
Juneau.
Juneau who?
Juneau the capital of Alaska?

❖ ❖ ❖

Knock, knock.
Who's there?
Buck and Ham.
Buck and Ham who?
Buck and Ham palace.

❖ ❖ ❖

Knock, knock.
Who's there?
Ali.
Ali who?
Ali Bama.

 ❖ ❖ ❖

Knock, knock.
Who's there?
Adele.
Adele who?
Adele is where the farmer's in.

❖ ❖ ❖

Knock, knock.
Who's there?
A herd.
A herd who?
A herd you were home, so I came over!

Who Is It?

Knock, knock.
Who's there?
Whittle.
Whittle who?
Whittle Orphan Annie.

❖ ❖ ❖

Knock, knock.
Who's there?
Tarzan.
Tarzan who?
Tarzan Stripes Forever.

❖ ❖ ❖

Knock, knock.
Who's there?
Specter.
Specter who?
Specter Holmes of Scotland Yard.

Knock, knock.
Who's there?
Soup.
Soup who?
Superman.

Knock, knock.
Who's there?
Olmen.
Olmen who?
Olmen River, that Olmen River...

Knock, knock.
Who's there?
Gable.
Gable who?
Gable to leap tall buildings in a single bound!

Knock, knock.
Who's there?
Esther.
Esther who?
Esther a doctor in the house?

Knock, knock.
Who's there?
Gravy.
Gravy who?
Gravy Crockett.

Knock, knock.
Who's there?
Diploma.
Diploma who?
Diplomas here to fix your leaky pipes.

Knock, knock.
Who's there?
Cologne.
Cologne who?
Cologne Ranger!

Knock, knock.
Who's there?
Atom.
Atom who?
Atom N. Eve.

❖ ❖ ❖

Knock, knock.
Who's there?
Archer.
Archer who?
Archer mother and father at home?

❖ ❖ ❖

Knock, knock.
Who's there?
Amanda.
Amanda who?
Amanda fix your washing machine.

❖ ❖ ❖

Knock, knock.
Who's there?
Alex.
Alex who?
Alex in Wonderland!

❖ ❖ ❖

Knock, knock.
Who's there?
Ezra.
Ezra who?
Ezra a doctor in the house?

Knock, knock.
Who's there?
Abe Lincoln.
Abe Lincoln who?
Don't you know who Abe Lincoln is?

Knock, knock.
Who's there?
Adam.
Adam who?
Adam my way, I'm coming in!

Knock, knock.
Who's there?
Alison.
Alison who?
Alison Wonderland.

Knock, knock.
Who's there?
Adam.
Adam who?
Adam up and get the total.

Knock, knock.
Who's there?
Amarillo.
Amarillo who?
Amarillo fashioned cowboy.

Knock, knock.
Who's there?
Avon.
Avon who?
The Avon lady. Your doorbell isn't working.

Knock, knock.
Who's there?
Amaryllis.
Amaryllis who?
Amaryllis state agent. Wanna buy a house?

You Said It!

Knock, knock.
Who's there?
Gladys.
Gladys who?
Gladys summer.

Knock, knock.
Who's there?
Gus.
Gus who?
Gus you don't want to play with me.

Knock, knock.
Who's there?
Heidi.
Heidi who?
Heidi Ho!

❖ ❖ ❖

Knock, knock.
Who's there?
Missouri.
Missouri who?
Missouri loves company!

❖ ❖ ❖

Knock, knock.
Who's there?
Dick.
Dick who?
Dick 'em up! This is a holdup.

❖ ❖ ❖

Knock, knock.
Who's there?
Disjoint.
Disjoint who?
Disjoint is closed.

❖ ❖ ❖

Knock, knock.
Who's there?
November.
November who?
November when we used to hate knock-knock jokes?

Knock, knock.
Who's there?
Anita Loos.
Anita Loos who?
Anita Loos about 10 pounds.

Knock, knock.
Who's there?
Alison.
Alison who?
Alison to the radio.

Knock, knock.
Who's there?
Augusta.
Augusta who?
Augusta wind blew my hat off!

Knock, knock.
Who's there?
Yukon.
Yukon who?
Yukon say that again.

Knock, knock.
Who's there?
Vera.
Vera who?
Vera interesting.

Knock, knock.
Who's there?
Uruguay.
Uruguay who?
You go Uruguay, and I'll go mine.

Knock, knock.
Who's there?
Turnip.
Turnip who?
Turnip the heat; it's cold in this house.

Knock, knock.
Who's there?
Toyota.
Toyota who?
Toyota be a law against knock-knock jokes.

Knock, knock.
Who's there?
Sum Toi.
Sum Toi who?
Sum Toi you've got there.

Knock, knock.
Who's there?
Sherwood.
Sherwood who?
Sherwood be good if someone did away with
    knock-knock jokes.

Knock, knock.
Who's there?
Roseanne.
Roseanne who?
Roseanne the tulip are my favorite flowers.

Other Books by Bob Phillips

The All-New Clean Joke Book

The Awesome Book
of Bible Trivia

Awesome Book
of Heavenly Humor

Awesome Dinosaur Jokes
for Kids

Awesome Good Clean Jokes
for Kids

The Best of the Good
Clean Jokes

Controlling Your Emotions
Before They Control You

Dude, Got Another Joke?

Extremely Good Clean
Jokes for Kids

How Can I Be Sure?

Over the Hill & On a Roll

Over the Next Hill
& Still Rolling

Personal Prayer List

Squeaky Clean Jokes for Kids

Super Cool Jokes
and Games for Kids

Super-Duper Good
Clean Jokes for Kids

A Tackle Box
of Fishing Funnies

Totally Cool Clean
Jokes for Kids

The World's Greatest
Collection of Clean Jokes

The World's Greatest
Collection of Knock-Knock
Jokes for Kids

For more information, send a self-addressed stamped envelope to:

Family Services
P.O. Box 9363
Fresno, California 93702